HALFPENNY (

Postcards from Barnes & Mortlake

ERRATA

P42, Plate 81 and P61, Plate 117
United Reformed Church should read
BARNES METHODIST CHURCH
P39, Plate 75 1930's should read 1950's.

ACKNOWLEDGEMENTS

The Barnes and Mortlake History Society wishes to thank the following for the loan of photographic material and for their kind permission to reproduce it here:

Mrs Marion Brackpool, Mrs Maisie Brown, Mr David Catford, Mr Graeme Cruickshank, Mr Leslie Freeman, Mr Raymond Gill, Miss Mary Grimwade, Dr David Redstone, and The Barnes, Mortlake and Sheen Times.

The captions were written by Miss Mary Grimwade and Mr David Catford and typed by Mrs Valerie Knight.

—

HALFPENNY GREEN

Postcards from Barnes and Mortlake

COMPILED BY THE PUBLICATIONS SUB-COMMITTEE
BARNES AND MORTLAKE HISTORY SOCIETY, 1994

© *Barnes and Mortlake History Society 1994*

First published in 1994
by Barnes and Mortlake History Society
and
Picton Publishing (Chippenham) Limited
ISBN 0 948251 78 6

Set in Linotype Bembo by
Mike Kelly Phototypesetting,
Biddestone, Chippenham, Wiltshire SN14 7EA
Printed and Bound in the United Kingdom by
Picton Publishing (Chippenham) Limited
Queensbridge Cottages,
Patterdown,
Chippenham,
Wiltshire SN15 2NS
Telephone: (0249) 443430

CONTENTS

COAT OF ARMS
OF THE OLD
BOROUGH OF BARNES

INTRODUCTION

1994 marked the Centenary of the Postcard which in its various forms can be one of the most evocative means of written communication. As a picture postcard, not only can the often brief message bring back memories of places and events but also the illustration can serve as a reminder of the ever-changing world around us.

The earliest use of postcards provided a quick and effective means of correspondence, with space for the written message confined to the same side as the partial illustration, and the entire reverse side reserved for the address. It was only in more recent years that the familiar pattern of the whole of one side devoted to a picture, with correspondence and the address on reverse side, was introduced.

For the then standard ½d postage rate the earliest cards could be posted and delivered within a certain distance on the same day as written, there being several deliveries of mail on each weekday. An invitation to afternoon tea on the same day was then quite possible. For 1d postage a similar card could even be mailed to a foreign destination.

To the local historian picture postcards offer a unique source of recorded detail that would otherwise be lost in the passage of time. The efforts of amateur photographers to record local scenes and events at a particular time are all too often lost to succeeding generations. The postcard, therefore, remains as a significant record of the past and a constant reminder of the inevitable changes that have occurred during earlier decades.

For this publication a representative range of postcards and promotional matter have been selected which are considered to be of general interest to those in our locality and elsewhere. Their selection entailed painstaking consideration of the several hundred items retained in the Society's archives and in the possession of members, to whom we are greatly indebted

David Catford

HOUSES

1. – *c.* 1910. THE LARGE PRIVATE HOUSE ON LEFT SIDE WAS THRELKELD HOUSE – IT IS NOW THE SITE OF SEAFORTH LODGE

2. – THIS HOUSE STOOD AT THE END OF ELLISON ROAD. BUILT *c.* 1868 IT WAS BOMBED IN 1940 AND THEN DEMOLISHED.

3. – CLEVELAND HOUSE, BARNES GREEN, *c.* 1885 WITH MEMBERS OF THE WILKINSON FAMILY.

Having acquired this old World property, W. G. JULIAN invites his customers and friends to view the house and grounds which he is using for the display of ANTIQUES in their various forms and contemporary surroundings and being able to economise in his expenses is offering GENUINE ANTIQUES at MODERATE PRICES.

Please give a look in.

Tel. 963 Hammersmith.

"THE GRANGE," CHURCH ROAD, BARNES, S.W.

4. – *c.* 1730. NOW A HOME FOR ELDERLY PEOPLE UNDER THE AUSPICES OF RICHMOND–UPON–THAMES HOUSING TRUST. THIS CARD *c.* 1920.

5. – Canon kitson stands by the greenhouse formerly in the barnes rectory garden *c.* 1910.

6. – The rosary (trock's mill cottage) mill hill, barnes *c.* 1905.

3

7. – Now strawberry house. Early 20th century card

8. – Garden of essex house. dr. and mrs henry hamilton on right hand side. *c.* 1920.

4

9. – FRONT VIEW OF ESSEX HOUSE, BARNES. BUILT *c.* 1850. THIS CARD *c.* 1920.

10. – OLD CROMWELL HOUSE, MORTLAKE. THE ENTRANCE FRONT OF THE ANCIENT HOUSE WHICH
STOOD IN AYNSCOMBE LANE. EDWARD COLSTON, LOCAL PHILANTHROPIST, DIED HERE 1731. HOUSE
DEMOLISHED 1857.

11. – Marsham lodge, high st. mortlake. this ancient house stood beside the white hart facing the broadway. it was demolished for road widening in 1930.

12. –The limes in mortlake high street served as the council premises until the formation of the london borough of richmond–upon–thames.

card dated ju 27 1911:

"You can feel quite comfortable about the children, they have not all been chucked out."

13. – BUILT 1727 WHITE LODGE IN RICHMOND PARK HAS BEEN THE HOME OF A NUMBER OF MEMBERS OF THE ROYAL FAMILY. IT NOW HOUSES THE ROYAL BALLET SCHOOL.

14. – THE SITE OF THIS IMPORTANT SHEEN HOUSE IS NOW OCCUPIED BY HOMES IN SHEEN LANE, SHREWSBURY AVENUE AND RICHMOND PARK ROAD. *c.* 1904

15. – The vicarage, vicarage road, east sheen. Early 20th century. Now renamed mortlake house.

16. – The one time home of the duke and duchess of fife. The house and grounds are now occupied by york and hood avenues.

card dated nov 9, 1912:
"I am quite looking forward to my visit to 'The Cherub' tomorrow evening."

17. – LONSDALE ROAD. IN 1910 THESE SCHOOLGIRLS WITH THEIR HOCKEY STICKS WERE PROBABLY PUPILS AT CASTELNAU COLLEGE, A FEW DOORS AWAY.

18. – ROSSLYN AVENUE c.1920, BUT BUILT ABOUT 7 YEARS EARLIER.

19. –The crescent. this shows the priory in the background which was demolished *c.*1916.

20. – Glebe road. these houses were built on former glebe lands in 1896.

21. – *c.* 1900. SHOPS STOOD NEXT DOOR TO THE SUN INN WHERE THE CAR PARK IS SITUATED. THIS CARD WAS PRINTED IN GERMANY.

22. – NOTE THE ABSENCE OF A RIVER WALL.

23. – THE HOUSE ON THE SITE ON WHICH THIS ROAD WAS BUILT IN 1904 WAS BYFIELD HOUSE, BUT THE ROAD IS KNOWN AS BYFELD GARDENS.

"Dear mother,

Made a cake for you but oven too hot,so alas effect quite spoilt, so have only sent you a morsel to inspect. Shall be up this evening for supper. Had a very good time last night.

What do you think of p.c.? Do you see little Marjorie with the maid outside the house, best love from us both, May.

Am rather ashamed to send the cake, it is so very badly cooked."

24. – KITSON ROAD, BUILT 1907, WAS NAMED AFTER THE RECTOR, CANON B.M.KITSON. THE LAND HAD PREVIOUSLY BEEN THE RECTORY PADDOCK.

25. – ROADMAKING AT RIVERVIEW GARDENS, BARNES. 29 MARCH, 1907.

26. – c.1910, THE ROW OF HOUSES ON THE RIGHT HAND SIDE WERE NAMED CHURCH TERRACE AS THEY WERE CLOSE TO HOLY TRINITY CHURCH.

27. – THESE FLATS ADJOINING HAMMERSMITH BRIDGE REMAIN THE SAME AS WHEN THEY WERE BUILT
AT THE TURN OF THE CENTURY.

28. – MADRID ROAD WAS LAID OUT TN 1906. SIR GERARD LOWTHER, OWNER OF THE LAND HAD
SERVED IN THE DIPLOMATIC CORPS IN MADRID.

29. – BUILT *c.*1913 THIS ROAD AND OTHERS ON THE ESTATE WERE KNOWN AS THE WHITE CITY AS THEIR WHITE STUCCO FACADES WERE REMINDERS OF THE EXHIBITION CENTRE AT SHEPHERD'S BUSH.

29A – C. 1898. BUILT ON GLEBE LAND, NAMED AFTER CANON B. MEREDYTH KITSON.

30. – LEINSTER AVENUE, LOOKING TOWARDS UPPER RICHMOND ROAD WITH GERALDINE VILLAS IN DISTANCE.

31. – AT JUNCTION OF MARTINDALE WITH CHRISTCHURCH ROAD.

32. – DERBY ROAD LOOKING NORTH. STONEDALE COTTAGE, OPPOSITE END OF ROAD, WAS OCCUPIED BY CHARLES CLIFFORD UNTIL 1923. IT THEN BECAME BARKERS ESTATE OFFICE FOR HOUSES BUILT ON LAND TO THE NORTH OF UPPER RICHMOND ROAD, FROM THERE TO SHEEN COURT AND BACKING ON TO THE RAILWAY, FORMERLY MARKET GARDENS WORKED BY BARKER FAMILY.

33. – PALEWELL PARK *c.*1904 WITH CORNER OF PARK AVENUE ON RIGHT.

17

34. – COVAL ROAD LOOKING NORTH. NOTE THE HOUSES IN CARLTON ROAD AND ADVERTISEMENT HOARDINGS ON UPPER RICHMOND ROAD.

35. – ONLY THE JOLLY GARDENERS REMAINS, ALBEIT NOW OVERSHADOWED BY DEVELOPMENT OF THE BREWERY. LANCING TERRACE WAS DEMOLISHED IN 1960's.

36. – Hertford Avenue looking south from Upper Richmond Road.

3 or 4
BED,
2 RECEPT.
OFFICES.

—

Every Labour
Saving device

Leases 99 yrs.
G. R. £8 8s.
Price, £   .
— 990
If desired
£200 Cash,
Balance as
Rent.

Apply—

C. & E. MELVILLE,
EAST SHEEN.

PHONE: RICHMOND 1352.

THE BARKER ESTATE, E. SHEEN, s.w.14.

GROUND FLOOR

FIRST FLOOR

37. – Burdenshott Avenue, Warren Avenue and Tangier Road were built on land acquired
by the last large scale market gardeners in East Sheen c.1927.

CLARE LAWN ESTATE, EAST SHEEN

ADJOINING
RICHMOND PARK.

ATTRACTIVE
DETACHED and
SEMI-DETACHED
RESIDENCES.

Prices:
£2,000 to £2,500
FREEHOLD.

Telephones:
Richmond 1839 and 3077,

Sole Agents: **ROSEVEARS, F.A.I.,** SURVEYORS, at OFFICE ON ESTATE,
AND 335 UPPER RICHMOND ROAD, EAST SHEEN, S.W. 14.

38. – A 1925 ADVERTISEMENT CARD FOR HOUSES BUILT ON THE SITE OF CLARE LAWN, THE FORMER RESIDENCE OF FREDERICK WIGAN. BUILT FOR HIM IN 1866.

39. – EAST SHEEN AVENUE 1905, LOOKING NORTH TOWARDS UPPER RICHMOND ROAD WAS FORMERLY KNOWN AS TITTLEBURY HILL AND NICKNAMED SHADY LANE BY REASON OF THE FINE PLANE TREES.

40. – MORTLAKE HIGH STREET LOOKING WEST TOWARDS THE BREWERY. WALL OF ST. MARY'S CHURCH AT EXTREME LEFT.

41. – LOOKING TOWARDS THE BREWERY WITH THE QUEEN'S HEAD ON THE RIGHT.

42. – COWLEY MANSIONS, MORTLAKE HIGH STREET. THESE FLATS BUILT 1910. PHOTOGRAPH TAKEN EARLY 1920'S.

43. – GRAEMESDYKE AVENUE. THIS ESTATE WAS BEING CONSTRUCTED IN 1908 PHOTOGRAPH TAKEN *c.*1912.

44. – GILPIN AVENUE. BUILT 1909, PHOTOGRAPH TAKEN *c*.1912

45. – JUNCTION WITH SHEEN LANE – WALL OF THE ANGLES ON LEFT. PHOTO *c*. 1920.

46. – AVONDALE ROAD, HOUSES BUILT *c.*1900. PHOTOGRAPH TAKEN *c.*1910.

47. – ASHLEIGH ROAD.HOUSES BUILT *c.*1900. PHOTOGRAPH TAKEN *c.*1910.

48. – SHEEN LANE. *c.*1920. NOTE BARCLAYS BANK (FORMERLY LONDON AND SOUTH WESTERN BANK) NOW R.E.COTES.

49. – LOOKING WEST *c.*1930. BUILT AT THE BEGINNING OF THE 20TH CENTURY

50. – Temple Sheen Road, formerly known as Blind Lane. Back of Geraldine Villas in distance.

51. – The Triangle, otherwise known as Milestone Green. The Picturedrome opened on Boxing Day, 1910 and it is believed that only silent films were shown there during its 19 years of existence. It was replaced by the Sheen Kinema (Odeon) in 1930.

52. – UPPER RICHMOND ROAD WEST.*c*.1908. IVY COTTAGE (A DOCTOR'S HOUSE) ON RIGHT.

52A – FEOM "THE COURT GUIDE" 1872.

TELEPHONE : No. 531 PUTNEY.

W. GLENIE, BUTCHER,

127, Church Road, and 194, Castelnau, BARNES. S.W.

FAMILIES SUPPLIED.   Southdown, Scotch, Dartmoor and Welsh Mutton.
Highland, Scot and Aberdeen Beef of the Best Quality.   Home-killed Meat.   Farm at
HEATHROW, Middx.   Home-made Beef and Pork Sausages.   Dairy Fed Pork.
Canterbury Lamb a Speciality.

53. – FAMILY BUTCHER, FROM THE OFFICIAL GUIDE OF 1909.

The
Men's
Wear
Shop

◻ ◻

67.
HIGH ST.
BARNES.

54. – A.E.CUFF & CO. – A LONG ESTABLISHED BARNES RETAILER. MR. CUFF'S PREMISES WERE LATER
TO BE FOUND IN CHURCH ROAD.

55. – 52, WHITE HART LANE *c.*1921 (MORTLAKE SIDE).

56. – BARNES HIGH STREET *c.*1910, ROSE HOUSE, A BUILDER'S MERCHANT STORE ON EXTREME RIGHT.

57. – Barnes High Street c.1900. The semi–detached houses on the left were Cottesmore villas, now shops. Threlkeld House was beyond them, now the site of Seaforth Lodge.

58. – Church Road, Barnes c.1900. The church wall is on the left, opposite is the entrance to Priory Lodge, home of actor–manager Edward Terry.

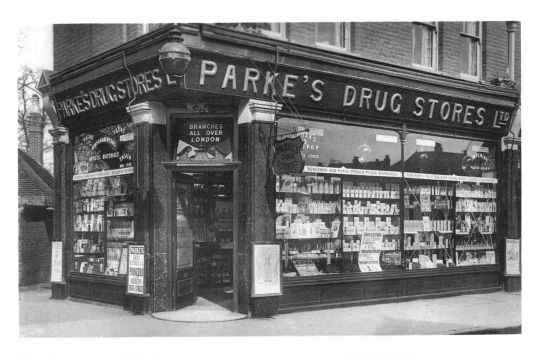

59. – SHEEN LANE *c.*1920. CORNER OF UPPER RICHMOND AND MILTON ROADS.

REVERSE OF CARD AN ADVERTISEMENT:
   "This photograph is printed on a Parke's Bromide Post Card."

60. – *c.*1920. CORNER OF PALEWELL PARK LOOKING TOWARDS SHEEN LANE CROSS ROADS.

61. – SHEEN LANE *c.*1920. THE RAILINGS ON RIGHT WERE THE BORDER OF MORTLAKE GREEN

62. – BARNES HIGH STREET ROSE HOUSE ON EXTREME RIGHT.

CARD DATED MARCH 11, 1908:
    "Shall be home usual time on Saturday, Bert".

63. – c.1920. ENTRY INTO HIGH STREET FROM BARNES TERRACE. NOTE THE SPEED LIMIT FOR MOTOR VEHICLES.

64. – c.1918. THE SHOPS WERE ORIGINALLY THE COTTAGES KNOWN AS CHURCH ROW.

65. – CASTLENAU, BARNES *c.* 1920 SHOPS IN THE VICINITY OF THE 'BOILEAU ARMS'.

66. – *c.*1925. MILTON ROAD CORNER ON RIGHT, ST.LEONARDS ROAD ON LEFT.

67. – *c.*1924. THORNE TERRACE SHOPS ENDING ON CORNER OF ARCHWAY STREET.

68. – *c.*1916. LOOKING EAST. THE 'OLD GEORGE' HAS BEEN REBUILT AS 'THE CHARLIE BUTLER'.

69. – July 1988. Evans supply stores, Barnes high street. This shop opened in 1905 owned by the same family it served the area continuously until its closure after 80 years.

70. – c.1930. The road on the right is Coval Road.

71. – *c*.1925. Looking east. Portman Avenue on left hand side.

72. – *c*.1920. The last word in modern living.

YOU can ELECTRIFY your Home step by step, LIGHTING now—FLAT-IRON, KETTLE, FAN and BED WARMER as required, FIRES for occasional use, COOKING RANGE to follow, VACUUM SWEEPER and WASHING MACHINE whenever convenient.

The appliances are self-contained. Their position does not depend on flue or structure. Place them wherever they are of most use and convenience and there they will perform their functions and save much laborious housework.

Cooking by ELECTRICITY saves waste of food and gives ideal meals with the minimum demand on time and attention. ELECTRICITY cuts out those bug-bears of the housewife, coal fires, the source of dirt, and dust, and the cause for frequent house cleanings with all their accompanying evils.

73. – St. Mary's, Barnes *c.*1904. Before the addition of the north aisle. This card was printed in Germany.

74. – *c.* 1904 Holy Trinity, Castlenau, Barnes. This card printed in Dresden. states : '½d stamp inland, foreign 1d.'

75. – BUILT IN THE 1930's THIS CHURCH REPLACED A FORMER TEMPORARY HUT–LIKE ERECTION WHICH HAD SERVED THE BARNES CATHOLICS WHO OTHERWISE HAD TO ATTEND THE MORTLAKE CHURCH.
A RAPHAEL TUCK CARD 'To bring you greetings'

76. – ST.MICHAEL'S CHURCH, ELM BANK GARDENS, BARNES WAS CONSECRATED JAN 26 1893. IT WAS THEN A DAUGHTER CHURCH UNDER THE CARE OF THE RECTOR OF BARNES. THIS CARD OF 16.1.07 SAYS : "I cannot imagine how I missed you last night. Anyway, will see you tomorrow at the time you mention."

77. – MORTLAKE PARISH CHURCH, MORTLAKE HIGH STREET. THIS 1543 BUILDING HAS UNDERGONE EXTENSIVE ALTERATIONS AND ENLARGEMENT DURING ITS LONG HISTORY. IT REPLACED AN EARLIER CHAPEL ERECTED IN 1348 DURING THE REIGN OF EDWARD III ON A SITE NOW COVERED BY THE ORIGINAL BREWERY COMPLEX. "Bert and I were married here on the 26th August, 1911."

78. – ALL SAINTS, EAST SHEEN CONSECRATED ON ALL SAINTS' DAY 1929, THE CHURCH WAS BUILT ON LAND BEQUEATHED UNDER THE WILL OF MAJOR SHEPHERD-CROSS, M.P. FOR BOLTON WHO LIVED AT NEARBY PALEWELL LODGE FROM 1896 UNTIL HIS DEATH IN 1913. THE FOUNDATION STONE WAS LAID BY H.R.H. DUCHESS OF YORK, NOW QUEEN ELIZABETH, THE QUEEN MOTHER ON OCTOBER 28TH 1928.

79. – St. Mary Magdalene r.c. church, north worple way. built *c.* 1851 on land where cows had been kept by mr lund, a local milkman,

80. – Built on land formerly part of farm at entrance to sheen common, consecration of the church on 13th january 1864 had been delayed for nine months following collapse of the tower when nearing completion.

81. – THIS CHURCH, NOW THE UNITED REFORMED WAS BUILT 1906.

CARD OF 1910 SAYS:
  "Sorry to have just missed post. I expect you will get this on Monday. Au revoir until then."

82. – THIS CHURCH WAS THE FORERUNNER OF THE WESLEYAN CHURCH IN STATION ROAD. IT IS NOW USED AS A HEALING CENTRE IN WHITE HART LANE.

83. – LONSDALE ROAD BOYS' SCHOOL BARNES *c.*1914. HEADMASTER MR. RAWLINSON, MISTRESS MISS BAILEY.

84. – BARNES GREEN SCHOOL WAS THE NATIONAL SCHOOL, DATING FROM 1850. AT ONE TIME BOYS, GIRLS AND INFANTS WERE TAUGHT UNDER ITS ROOF.

Convent Grounds shewing refectory,
Convent of Sacred Heart,
45, Church Road, Barnes, S.W.

85. – THE CONVENT SCHOOL BEGAN *c*.1905 AND CONTINUED WITH DAY AND BOARDING PUPILS UNTIL 1969. THE NUNS WERE A FRENCH COMMUNITY AND DID MOST OF THE TEACHING. PRINTED IN SAXONY.

The Chapel,
Convent of the Sacred Heart,
45, Church Road, Barnes, S.W.

86. – THE NUNS' CHAPEL BUILT AT. THE SIDE OF 45, CHURCH ROAD AND NOW A SCHOOL ROOM. PRINTED IN SAXONY.

87. – DATED AP.11,1905. FORMERLY CASTELNAU HOUSE IT STOOD BESIDE THE RIVER AT THE END OF ASHLEIGH ROAD AND WAS A GIRLS'SCHOOL BEFORE ITS DEMOLITION AT THE AT THE TURN OF THETWENTIETH CENTURY

Temple Grove.

88. – c.1902.THIS FAMOUS BOYS' PREPARATORY SCHOOL WAS HOUSED IN SHEEN DURING THE GREATER PART OF THE 19TH CENTURY. IT LATER MOVED TO SUSSEX WHERE IT CONTINUES TO FLOURISH.

89. – Castlenau College, Castlenau, Barnes. Mrs. Florence Pennington started this school c.1907 at 8–10 Lonsdale Road. After the 1st World War she moved to 45 Castelnau, finally retiring in the 1950's.

90. – LOWER RICHMOND ROAD *c.*1920. THESE SCHOOLS DEMOLISHED IN THE 1980'S. SITE NOW USED FOR COUNCIL HOUSING.

91. – SOUTH WEST LONDON COLLEGE. 1906–1932. 99–101, CASTELNAU, BARNES. HEADMASTER ERNEST BURBIDGE, B.A. LONDON. MRS. BURBIDGE ON LEFT OF HEAD. ERROL FLYNN PROBABLY 4TH BOY FROM LEFT, 2ND ROW.

RED LION HOTEL,

CASTELNAU, BARNES.   Proprietor, T. A. BROOKS.

CONCERTS HELD IN THE GROUNDS FROM EASTER TILL SEPTEMBER.
REFRESHMENTS served in the Grounds, including LUNCHEONS and TEAS.

92. – "AL FRESCO" CONCERTS, SUMMER 1909. AT THE RED LION, BARNES.

93. – 1904. THE RAILWAY TAVERN. ROEHAMPTON LANE ON LEFT. THIS CARD WAS PRINTED IN SAXONY.

94. – *c.*1920. THE BULL. UPPER RICHMOND ROAD, WEST. THIS WAS BUILT IN 1792 ON THE SITE OF A
17TH CENTURY INN. REBUILT 1938, DEMOLISHED 1987

95. – THE BULL, DEMOLITION IN 1938. CARD PRINTED IN ENGLISH AND FRENCH.

96. – THE RAILWAY TAVERN, SHEEN LANE, BECAME AN INN AFTER THE COMING OF THE RAILWAY. PREVIOUSLY THE HOUSE OF A POOR– RATE COLLECTOR IN NAPOLEONIC TIMES.

97. – c.1920. THE SUN INN, BARNES POND.

98. – *c.*1920. THE BULL'S HEAD. REBUILT IN 1847. FORMERLY THE KING'S HEAD IN 1737. WATERMAN'S ARMS. BUILT *c.*1850 ON SITE OF A BLACKSMITH'S FORGE.

99. – *c.*1920. THE MARKET GARDENER. THIS ROADWAY WAS KNOWN AS HOGGER'S CORNER.

100. – *c.*1920. THE RED LION HOTEL, BARNES

101. – *c.*1900. THE EDINBURGH CASTLE. CORNER OF ARCHWAY STREET AND WHITE HART LANE, BARNES.

"Hare and Hounds." Sheen.

102. – *c.*1900. THE HARE AND HOUNDS, UPPER RICHMOND ROAD, WAS SO NAMED IN 1776.

The White Hart, Barnes.

103. – *c.* 1900 NOTE THE HORSE-DRAWN BUS AND MARSHAM LODGE, WHICH WAS DEMOLISHED IN 1930.

104. – *c.*1910. THE COACH AND HORSES, BARNES HIGH STREET, COTTAGES ON LEFT HAND SIDE WERE DEMOLISHED FOR POLICE GARAGE.

105. – *c.*1915. THE LORD NAPIER, MORTLAKE HIGH STREET

106. – *c*.1908. THE TWO BREWERS, MORTLAKE HIGH STREET.

107. – *c*.1908. THIS INN STANDS AT THE CORNER OF SHIP LANE AND LOWER RICHMOND ROAD.

108. – *c.*1924. PULLED DOWN FOR ROAD WIDENING, AND NOW THE 'CHARLIE BUTLER'.

109. – *c.*1916. THE PLOUGH, EAST SHEEN. THIS AREA IS VERY LITTLE ALTERED TODAY.

110. – *c*.1920. THE WHEATSHEAF. 1854–1963. SITE NOW PART OF THE SHEEN LANE CENTRE.

110A – AS A MID NINETEENTH CENTURY ALE HOUSE IT WAS KNOWN AS THE 'FIVE ALLS': A CLERGYMAN
(I PRAY FOR ALL), A BARRISTER (I PLEAD FOR ALL), A FARMER (I MAINTAIN ALL), THE KING (I FIGHT
FOR ALL) AND HIS SATANIC MAJESTY (I TAKE ALL). THIS HOUSE STOOD IN THE UPPER RICHMOND
ROAD, FACING ELM ROAD.

BARNES COMMON.

111. – 1911. Looking towards the crossroads from the bottom of the railway bridge. "I have just got home and want my tea with a passion. Glad all is so bright. your loving Gwen."

112. – Sheen Common Fife Road entrance. *c.* 1910. Here formerly was the pound for straying animals.

"This is for your album."

113. – 1902. THE ROAD ON THE LEFT BORDERING ON THE COMMON IS QUEEN'S RIDE. THAT ON THE RIGHT IS UPPER RICHMOND ROAD LOOKING TOWARDS PUTNEY. THIS CARD HAD BEEN PRINTED BEFORE THE BACK WAS DIVIDED FOR ADDRESS AND CORRESPONDENCE.

114. – 1913, THE HOUSE WITH THE TURRET IN SHEEN LANE WAS ONE OF THE LODGES TO CLARE LAWN. "You see we are really at Sheen. We expect Bert tomorrow eve, Wednesday."

115. – BARNES COMMON,1904. THE CROSSROADS. PRINTED IN DRESDEN.

116. – ENTRANCE TO PALEWELL COMMON FROM STONEHILL ROAD, EAST SHEEN.

117. – Beverley brook footbridge, late 19th century. Cleveland house shows on site of present united reformed church.

118. – *c.*1910. Barnes common cemetery, showing keeper's residence.

119. – c.1910. THE FENCING ON THE RIGHT WAS A CONTINUATION OF THE FOOTPATH PROM STONEHILL ROAD.

120. – ENTRANCE TO SHEEN COMMON FROM TEMPLE SHEEN.

121. – *c.*1900. Park entrance from Sheen Lane, Turning to Fife Road on right .

122. – Mortlake Green, note the keeper who was responsible for maintenance.

123. – A COLD WINTER AT THE TURN OF THE CENTURY.

124. – SHEEN LANE. CORONATION DAY JUNE 22ND, 1911. WALKING TO SHEEN HOUSE TO ENJOY SPORTS,
TEA AND LATER AN EVENING DANCE

125 – 2ND MORTLAKE BOY SCOUTS PARADING OUTSIDE THE H.Q. IN ALDER ROAD IN 1923.

125A – A SKIFF ON THE RIVER BY THE WHITE HART LANDING STAGE.

126 – From 1925–7 Barnes Theatre was under the direction of Philip Ridgeway. Here famous actors and actresses appeared, including John Gielgud, Jean Forbes-Robertson, Ion Swinley Gwen Ffrangcon-Davies, and Charles Laughton. The building, better known as the Byfeld Hall, now houses the Olympic Recording Studios.

GWEN FFRANGCON-DAVIES in
TESS OF THE D'URBERVILLES

BARNES THEATRE
(OPPOSITE RANELAGH)
Licensee and Director ... ... PHILIP RIDGEWAY

'PHONE : RIVERSIDE 3701 (3 LINES)

Commencing MON., SEPT. 7th at 8.15
MATINEES Thursday and Saturday at 2.30
PHILIP RIDGEWAY
PRESENTS
TESS OF THE D'URBERVILLES
BY
THOMAS HARDY
GWEN FFRANGCON-DAVIES
(By arrangement with Sir Barry V. Jackson)

Ion Swinley	Austin Trevor
Stanley Lathbury	Margaret Carter
Drusilla Wills	Gabrielle Casartelli
C. Leveson Lane	John Le Hay

Post Card

The Address to be written on this side.

AFFIX STAMP HERE.

A Happy birthday with love from Walton

MB

127. – LOCAL REGATTAS WERE A FEATURE OF RIVERSIDE ACTIVITY UP TO WORLD WAR I.

128. – THE RED LION, BARNES. ENTRANCE TO THE FAMOUS RANELAGH CLUB WHERE POLO WAS THE SPORT OF KINGS, OPENING IN 1895. IT CLOSED IN 1939.

129. – THIS POND, JUST INSIDE THE SHEEN ENTRANCE TO THE PARK INTRODUCED BOATS IN 1930. THEY WERE DISCONTINUED IN SEPT 1939. SHEEN COTTAGE, DEMOLISHED BY BOMBS IN WORLD WAR II, IS SHOWN IN THE BACKGROUND.

130. – . c.1950. THIS WAS LAID OUT ON THE SITE OF A FORMER MARKET GARDEN WHICH WAS BETWEEN THE TWO RAILWAY LINES

131. – THE COUNTRY FAIR, EAST SHEEN. 1914.

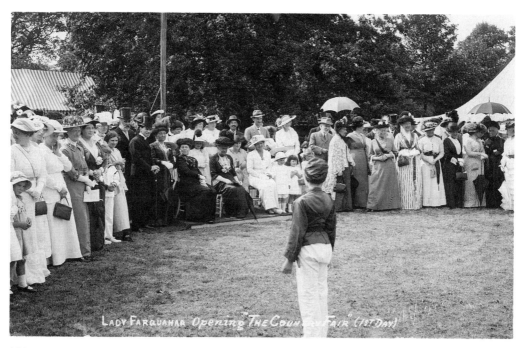

132. – EAST SHEEN LODGE GROUNDS, JULY 1914. LADY FARQUAHAR SEATED WITH SUNSHADE BETWEEN
HER KNEES

133. – *c.*1900. IMPORTANT GUESTS LEAVE THE RANELAGH CLUB.

134. – *c.*1920. A LOCAL SCOUT PATROL STANDS AT WHITE HART LANE LEVEL CROSSING.

BYFELD HALL,

BARNES.

Proprietor . . F. W. DUNKLEY.

THIS Hall has a seating accommodation of 500, is equipped with large stage and properties, allowing for the production of plays of modern requirements.

For Dancing the floor is second to none, accommodating 150 dancers with comfort. Adjoining is a smaller hall, suitable for private parties, whist drives, etc.

Both halls are heated throughout, and lighted by electricity, and are up to date in every detail.

The charges for hire are reasonable, being about half those of any Town Hall in London or Suburbs.

All communications to **BOX OFFICE.**

135, 136, — THE BYFELD HALL IN ITS EARLY DAYS AS A VENUE FOR DANCING AND FUNCTIONS.

The Two Brewers   The Gaiety Cinema

137. – THE GAIETY CINEMA, MORTLAKE. CLOSED IN 1930 AND DESTROYED BY FIRE IN 1961.

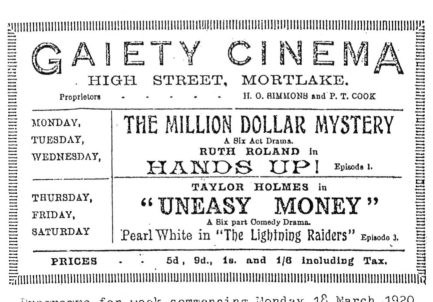

GAIETY CINEMA

HIGH STREET, MORTLAKE.

Proprietors - - - - - H. O. SIMMONS and P. T. COOK

MONDAY, TUESDAY, WEDNESDAY,	**THE MILLION DOLLAR MYSTERY** A Six Act Drama. **RUTH ROLAND in** **HANDS UP!** Episode 1.
THURSDAY, FRIDAY, SATURDAY	**TAYLOR HOLMES in** **"UNEASY MONEY"** A Six part Comedy Drama. Pearl White in "The Lightning Raiders" Episode 3.

PRICES - - 5d, 9d., 1s. and 1/6 including Tax.

Programme for week commencing Monday 18 March 1920

A famous landmark

Opposite the winning post of the Oxford and Cambridge Boat Race stands one of the oldest Breweries in England to-day—one which has been in continuous operation for over 450 years. This Brewery has been many times enlarged and is equipped with all the most up-to-date devices for brewing those ever popular beers—WATNEY'S ALES and REID'S STOUT.

WATNEY'S

Mortlake Brewery

138. – A FAMOUS LANDMARK

139. – Sheen House, Sheen Lane, the stables remain as offices on the corner of Shrewsbury avenue.

74

140. – 1907. CHILDREN PICNIC BY BARNES POND. THIS WAS ADDRESSED TO MRS. JEFFREYS, WARDROBE DEALER, ASKING HER: "To call tomorrow by 10 o'clock."

141. – c.1900. BEVERLEY BROOK AND BRIDGE.
   "Sorry, mater, will not be able to come. I will write soon, A.R."

142. – .Barnes common was renowned locally for pond dipping at the turn of the 19th/
20th century.

143. – *c.*1895. Barnes pond. Card printed after 1902.

144. – Inside Richmond Park with the wall in the distance, Beverley Brook.

145. – One of the several ponds in 1915 on Sheen Common.
 "Isn't this war awful. My boy has been missing since January. We were to have been married early this year. I hope he turns up alright. With love, Kitty.' card stamped 9.7.1915.

146. – Chiswick bridge from the Kew side during its construction, 1930–32. Card printed in English and French.

ROUND POND, EAST SHEEN

147. – This pond, now filled in, was at the entrance to Palewell Common.

BEVERLEY BROOK, BARNES.

D.1269

148. – THE BROOK FLOWS BETWEEN THE BRIDGE IN STATION ROAD AND THE FOOT BRIDGE ON THE COMMON.

4. RUSTIC BRIDGE. BARNES 18.

149. – *c.* 1910. THIS BRIDGE CROSSED THE RYTHE, A TRIBUTARY OF THE BEVERLEY BROOK, OPPOSITE ELM GROVE ROAD.

150. – THIS BOATHOUSE, MUCH USED BY OARSMEN, WAS UPSTREAM ON THE CHISWICK BANK FROM BARNES RAILWAY BRIDGE.

⌁ SURREY EDUCATION COMMITTEE. ⌁

THE THAMES AT BARNES BRIDGE.   E.S.A. LONDON. *Copyright.*

Never Absent, Never Late ....*Doris Bradley*....

151. – A REWARD FOR VIRTUE IN THE 1920'S.

BARNES FLOODS. 03.   MOYSE. Putney.

152. – THIS GREAT FLOOD OCCURRED IN JUNE 1903. THE BROOK AND POND OVERFLOWED DURING DAYS OF INCESSANT RAIN.

Very kind respects to your parents and friends. I shall shortly be with you: until then I wish you good health

Barnes (after heavy rainfall June 1903)   London

Dear Mr Brochet, I leave London tuesday evening arriving at Paris about 7½ in the morning. I shall leave St Lazare as soon as possible after that time. Do not trouble to get up earlier to come and meet me. We are certain to miss each other as I do not know the time

Gilbert Marlet, 116 High Street, Putney.

153. – THE BRIDGE IN STATION ROAD DURING THE JUNE FLOOD, 1903. THIS CARD WAS SENT TO VERSAILLES AND SO HAS A 1d. STAMP

154. – 25 AUGUST, 1907. COACH AND FOUR ON BARNES COMMON

155. – *c.*1904. SHEEN LANE LEVEL CROSSING.

156. – PRIOR TO 1916 WHEN THE LINE WAS ELECTRIFIED.

157. – c.1906. TRAIN NEAR VINE ROAD LEVEL CROSSING. BARNES STATION IN THE BACKGROUND.

157A – MOTORING OFFICIALLY RECOGNISED BY THE AUTHORITIES.

"In the early summer of 1900, the Automobile Club entertained the chief constables of counties to luncheon at Sheen House Club, Richmond, In addition to the hospitality, the guests were drive round Richmond Park and, later, were asked to state their views on the motor-car a a factor in public traffic".

158. – HAMMERSMITH BRIDGE WITH PIER AND STEAMER. 2.9.1906.

159. – 2.9.1906. HORSE BUS, HAMMERSMITH BRIDGE.

160. – *c.*1935. 395 CLASS NO 3167. NORTH WORPLE WAY ON LEFT.

BNS.13 THE RIVER THAMES, BARNES

COPYRIGHT
FRITH LTD

161. – THE TUG HAS LOWERED THE FUNNEL IN ORDER TO CLEAR BARNES BRIDGE.

162. – *c*.1910. Barnes terrace.

163. – 2.9.1906. Motor car, hammersmith bridge.

164. – THESE LEVEL CROSSING GATES WERE REMOVED IN OCTOBER 1975 AND THE SIGNAL BOX WAS DISMANTLED LATER.

165. – THE RIVER BEND SHOWING BREWERY BUILDINGS AND BARGES ON THE FORESHORE.

166. – The tall house and wooden shop were pulled down in 1971. The long ladder by signal post was used to light the oil lamps.

167. – Barnes station from the official guide of 1909.

168. – CHINESE TEA HOUSE, FORMERLY IN THE GROUNDS OF EAST SHEEN LODGE IS TRANSPORTED TO
THE SHEEN LAWN TENNIS CLUB. *c.*1926.

Photo by courtesy of J.Hickey (Richmond) Ltd.

169. – HORSE RE-FUELLING POINT, NEAR BARNES POND.

170. – ONE OF THE LAST BARGES IN COMMERCIAL USE ON THE THAMES.

171. – Horse riding on Barnes Terrace, *c.* 1900.

172. – Family coach of residents of "The Limes" Mortlake High Street, *c.* 1900.

173. – HORSE AND RIVER TRANSPORT, BARNES TERRACE.

174. – PADDLE STEAMER , *c.* 1910.

176. – One of the last "B" types at Mortlake bus garage, Avondale Road. Garage now demolished for housing development.

177. – "K" type motor bus, in use 1919–1932. In upper richmond road.

178. — Victorian wall box.

179. — Victorian Pillar Box.

180. – EDWARD VII PILLAR BOX.

181. – GEORGE V PILLAR BOX.